Dance Dance!

Lynn M Hayden

Other Books by the Author

Dancing For Him

Processionals, Props, & Pageantry

Dance In the Church, What's the Pointe?

Team Terrificus

Creative Worship

Divine Choreography

Prophetic Dance ~ Expressing His Heart

Dance Dance!

Lynn M. Hayden

Cover and Book Design: Jessica Mitchem
Book Production: SPS Publications, Eustis, Florida
www.spsbooks.com

ISBN-10: 0-9771925-3-9
ISBN-13: 978-0-9771925-3-3

DEDICATION

To the Lord—Who in the midst of us is mighty. Who will save.Who will *joy (Gil – To spin around under the influence of any violent emotion) over us with singing! (Zephaniah 3:17)*

To my wonderful husband, who is not only my co-laborer during ministry, but also is a continual support in all other areas of my life.

To Dashan Sardine who painstakingly took time to help me edit the fifth printing...thank you!

CONTENTS

Introduction 9

Dance Part I 11
English use of the word dance and its tenses
Clap. 13
Dance. 17

Dance Part II 23
Old Testament Hebrew words pertaining to movement
Barak. 25
Cabab. 27
Chagag 33
Chul, Chuwl, or Chil. 37
Dalag 41
Ealats or Ealaz. 43
Gil, Giyl, Gul, or Guwl. 45
Halal 53
Haliykah or Halijkah 63
Karar 65
Machowl or Machol 67
Macholah or Mechowlah. 69
Nathar 73
Pazaz 75
Raquad or Rekad. 77
Shachah 81
Shiyr 85
Tnuwphah 91
Towdah 97
Yadah 101

Dance part III 109
New Testament Greek words pertaining to movement
Agalliasis 111
Choros 113
Exallomai 115
Hallomai 117
Orcheomai .119
Prochorus .121
Proskuneo .123
Skirtao 127

Conclusion 129
Index 131
Bibliography 133
Contact Information 134

Introduction

It is and has been my heart, desire, and personal purpose to not only worship the Lord through the dance, and demonstrate the gospel of Jesus Christ through movement, but to also teach about its validity throughout the Bible, and impart it to others.

This book, although not exhaustive, is designed to educate the reader about the multitudinous references to dance and movement interspersed throughout the entire Bible. Not only does the Word contain the word dance and its derivatives, but also hundreds of words related to movement (which is what dance is).

It is important for any one who is called to the dance ministry, especially, to have a greater understanding of what we are doing when we dance before the Lord. However, anyone who has an interest or curiosity about movement ministry would greatly benefit from this resource.

My husband and I travel extensively and, much to my surprise, have discovered that many pastors, as well as laity, have never found dance in the church to be scriptural. Therefore, it is my hope that once people begin to read the Word, with a greater understanding (derived from this book), that their skepticism will be eradicated, and they will be able to embrace the dance as a valid form of worship, healing, and gospel presentation.

DANCE PART I
English Use of Words pertaining to movement

This section has an inclusive combination of scriptures from both the Old and New Testaments. Each scripture contains either the words "clap," "dance," or one of their tenses (or plurals) such as: danced, dances, or dancing. All the scriptures are in order according to how they are sequentially found in the Bible.

CLAP

Clap – to blow, strike or smite, sound, thrust, give a blow, blast; (Qal); to thrust, drive (of weapon); to give a blast, give a blow; to strike or clap hands; (Niphal); to be blown, blast (of horn); to strike or pledge oneself

The word clap has many different derivatives in the Hebrew. This is a compilation of several definitions to be shown as a general overview and not a thorough study. The many following scriptures that contain the word clap each have different derivatives are designed primarily to show you the multiple occurrences of the word.

OLD TESTAMENT

JOB

27:23 (Men) shall **clap** their hands at him, and shall hiss him out of his place.

PSALMS

47:1 (To the chief Musician, A Psalm for the sons of Korah.) O **clap** your hands, all ye people; shout unto God with the voice of triumph.

98:8 Let the floods **clap** (their) hands: let the hills be joyful together

ISAIAH

55:12 For ye shall go out with joy, and be led forth with peace: the mountains and the hills shall break forth before you into singing, and all the trees of the field shall **clap** (their) hands.

LAMENTATIONS

2:15 All that pass by **clap** (their) hands at thee; they hiss and wag their head at the daughter of Jerusalem, (saying, Is) this the city that (men) call The perfection of beauty, The joy of the whole earth?

NAHUM

3:19 (There is) no healing of thy bruise; thy wound is grievous: all that hear the bruit of thee shall **clap** the hands over thee: for upon whom hath not thy wickedness passed continually

DANCE

Dance, danced, dances, dancing – *To move the body and feet in rhythm, ordinarily to music; to move lightly and gaily; caper; to bob up and down; to be stirred into rapid movement, as leaves in a wind.*

OLD TESTAMENT

EXODUS

15:20: And Miriam the prophetess, the sister of Aaron, took a timbrel in her hand; and all the women went out after her with timbrels and with **dances**.

32:19: And it came to pass, as soon as he came nigh unto the camp, that he saw the calf, and the **dancing:** and Moses' anger waxed hot, and he cast the tables out of his hands, and brake them beneath the mount.

JUDGES

11:34: And Jephthah came to Mizpeh unto his house, and, behold, his daughter came out to meet him with timbrels and with **dances**: and she was his only child; beside her he had neither son nor daughter.

21:21: And see, and, behold, if the daughters of Shiloh come out to **dance in dances**, then come ye out of the vineyards, and catch you every man his wife of the daughters of Shiloh, and go to the land of Benjamin.

21:23: And the children of Benjamin did so, and took them wives, according to their number, of them that **danced**, whom they caught: and they went and returned unto their inheritance, and repaired the cities, and dwelt in them.

I SAMUEL

18:6: And it came to pass as they came, when David was returned from the slaughter of the Philistine, that the women came out of all cities of Israel, singing and **dancing**, to meet king Saul, with tabrets, with joy, and with instruments of musick.

21:11: And the servants of Achish said unto him, is not this David the king of the land? Did they not sing one to another of him in **dances**, saying, Saul hath slain his thousands, and David his ten thousands?

29:5: Is not this David, of whom they sang one to another in **dances**, saying, Saul slew his thousands, and David his ten thousands?

30:16: And when he had brought him down, behold, they were spread abroad upon all the earth, eating and drinking, and **dancing**, because of all the great spoil that they had taken out of the land of the Philistines, and out of the land of Judah.

II SAMUEL

6:14: And David **danced** before the LORD with all his might; and David was girded with a linen ephod.

6:16: And as the ark of the LORD came into the city of David, Michal Saul's daughter looked through a window, and saw king David leaping and **dancing** before the LORD; and she despised him in her heart.

I CHRONICLES

15:29: And it came to pass, as the ark of the covenant of the LORD came to the city of David, that Michal the daughter of Saul looking out at a window saw king David **dancing** and playing: and she despised him in her heart.

JOB

21:11: They send forth their little ones like a flock, and their children **dance**.

PSALMS

30:11: Thou hast turned for me my mourning into **dancing:** thou hast put off my sackcloth, and girded me with gladness.

149:3: Let them praise his name in the **dance**: let them sing praises unto him with the timbrel and harp.

150:4: Praise him with the timbrel and **dance**: praise him with stringed instruments and organs.

ECCLESIASTES

3:4: A time to weep, and a time to laugh; a time to mourn, and a time to **dance**.

ISAIAH

13:21: But wild beasts of the desert shall lie there; and their houses shall be full of doleful creatures; and owls shall dwell there, and satyrs shall **dance** there.

JEREMIAH

31:4: Again, I will build thee, and thou shalt be built, O virgin of Israel: thou shalt again be adorned with thy tabrets, and shalt go forth in the dances of them that make merry.

31:13: Then shall the virgin rejoice in the **dance**, both young men and old together: for I will turn their mourning into joy, and will comfort them, and make them rejoice from their sorrow.

LAMENTATIONS

5:15: The joy of our heart is ceased; our **dance** is turned into mourning.

NEW TESTAMENT

MATTHEW

14:6: But when Herod's birthday was kept, the daughter of Herodias **danced** before them, and pleased Herod.

MARK

6:22: And when the daughter of the said Herodias came in, and **danced**, and pleased Herod and them that sat with him, the king said unto the damsel, Ask of me whatsoever thou wilt, and I will give it thee.

LUKE

7:32: They are like unto children sitting in the marketplace, and calling one to another, and saying, We have piped unto you, and ye have not **danced**; we have mourned to you, and ye have not wept.

15:25: Now his elder son was in the field: and as he came and drew nigh to the house, he heard musick and **dancing.**

DANCE PART II
Old Testament Hebrew Words Pertaining to Dance or Movement

This section has quite a comprehensive compilation of scriptures related to movement. They are, first, listed in alphabetical order, according to the Hebrew word. Secondly, once each word is discovered, the related scriptures are in sequential order according to how they are found in the Bible.

The words found in bold capitalization, and in parentheses (next to or near the Hebrew word), are locator words extracted from that particular scripture. They are primarily listed in simplistic form, and are frequently found in the scripture in a different tense or plural. These are not necessarily the definition, however, they often overlap with the meaning.

Finally, the definition of the Hebrew word is found after the locator.

Example:

***HALAL – (Praise)** – To make a show, to be clamorously foolish…(shortened definition for example)*

I CHRONICLES

29:13 – Now therefore, our God, we thank thee, and **praise** thy glorious name.

We see that HALAL is the Hebrew word, followed by **PRAISE** (the scripture locator word). So when we read the scripture, and run across the word **praise** (or one of its tenses or plurals) we then understand that it means whatever its following definition is.

BARAK

BARAK – (Bless; Kneel) *To praise by kneeling or bowing down—an implication of blessing God with humility of heart in adoration.*

II CHRONICLES

6:13: For Solomon had made a brazen scaffold, of five cubits long, and five cubits broad, and three cubits high, and had set it in the midst of the court: and upon it he stood, and **kneeled** down upon his knees before all the congregation of Israel, and spread forth his hands toward heaven,

PSALMS

34:1: I will **bless** the LORD at all times: his praise shall continually be in my mouth.

63:4: Thus will I **bless** thee while I live: I will lift up my hands in thy name.

95:6: O come, let us worship and bow down: let us **kneel** before the LORD our maker.

134:3: The LORD that made heaven and earth **bless** thee out of Zion

CABAB

CABAB – **(Compass; Go About)** *To revolve, surround or border; to revolve around a sacred object; walk; whirl.*

GENESIS

19:4: But before they lay down, the men of the city, even the men of Sodom, **compassed** the house round, both old and young, all the people from every quarter:

NUMBERS

21:4: And they journeyed from mount Hor by the way of the Red sea, to **compass** the land of Edom: and the soul of the people was much discouraged because of the way.

34:5: And the border shall fetch a **compass** from Azmon unto the river of Egypt, and the goings out of it shall be at the sea.

DEUTERONOMY

2:1: Then we turned, and took our journey into the wilderness by the way of the Red sea, as the LORD spake unto me: and we **compassed** mount Seir many days.

2:3: Ye have **compassed** this mountain long enough: turn you northward.

JOSHUA

6:3: And ye shall **compass** the city, all ye men of war, and go round about the city once. Thus, shalt thou do six days.

6:11: So the ark of the LORD **compassed** the city, going about it once: and they came into the camp, and lodged in the camp.

6:14: And the second day they **compassed** the city once, and returned into the camp: so they did six days.

6:15: And it came to pass on the seventh day, that they rose early about the dawning of the day, and **compassed** the city after the same manner seven times: only on that day they **compassed** the city seven times.

15:3: And it went out to the south side to Maaleh-acrabbim, and passed along to Zin, and ascended up on the south side unto Kadesh-barnea, and passed along to Hezron, and went up to Adar, and fetched a **compass** to Karkaa:

II SAMUEL

5:23: And when David enquired of the LORD, he said, Thou shalt not go up; but fetch a **compass** behind them, and come upon them over against the mulberry trees.

I KINGS

7:15: For he cast two pillars of brass, of eighteen cubits high apiece: and a line of twelve cubits did **compass** either of them about.

7:23: And he made a molten sea, ten cubits from the one brim to the other: it was round all about, and his height was five cubits: and a line of thirty cubits did **compass** it round about.

II KINGS

3:9: So the king of Israel went, and the king of Judah, and the king of Edom: and they fetched a **compass** of seven days' journey: and there was no water for the host, and for the cattle that followed them.

II CHRONICLES

4:2: Also he made a molten sea of ten cubits from brim to brim, round in compass, and five cubits the height thereof; and a line of thirty cubits did **compass** it round about.

4:3: And under it was the similitude of oxen, which did **compass** it round about: ten in a cubit, compassing the sea round about. Two rows of oxen were cast, when it was cast.

JOB

40:22: The shady trees cover him with their shadow; the willows of the brook **compass** him about.

PSALMS

7:7: So shall the congregation of the people **compass** thee about: for their sakes therefore return thou on high.

26:6: I will wash mine hands in innocence: so will I **compass** thine altar, O LORD:

32:7: Thou art my hiding place; thou shalt preserve me from trouble; thou shalt **compass** me about with songs of deliverance. Selah.

32:10: Many sorrows shall be to the wicked: but he that trusteth in the LORD, mercy shall **compass** him about.

48:12: **Walk about** Zion, and go round about her: tell the towers thereof.

49:5: Wherefore should I fear in the days of evil, when the iniquity of my heels shall **compass** me about?

55:10: Day and night they **go about** it upon the walls thereof: mischief also and sorrow are in the midst of it.

59:14: And at evening, let them return; and let them make a noise like a dog, and **go round about** the city.

ECCLESIASTES

12:5: Also when they shall be afraid of that which is high, and fears shall be in the way, and the almond tree shall flourish, and the grasshopper shall be a burden, and desire shall fail: because man goeth to his long home, and the mourners **go about** the streets:

SONG OF SOLOMON

3:2: I will rise now, and **go about** the city in the streets, and in the broad ways I will seek him whom my soul loveth: I sought him, but I found him not.

JEREMIAH

52:21: And concerning the pillars, the height of one pillar was eighteen cubits; and a fillet of twelve cubits did **compass** it; and the thickness thereof was four fingers: it was hollow.

CHAGAG

CHAGAG – (Feast; keep; kept holy day; dancing)
A sacred celebration, marching in a sacred procession; to keep a feast; to be festive; assemble for rejoicing and celebration; reeling to and fro; dancing in sacred procession; to celebrate; to move in a circle; to dance; to make a pilgrimage; keep a pilgrim feast; to observe a festival; keep or hold a solemn feast or holiday; idea of leaping; A perfume (Qatar or Qetoreth—a fumigation that drives out the occupants and causes deliverance) of fire is released to God when praising Him in a holy procession. The result in the spirit realm is that when we offer praise to the Lord or when we "Chagag" Him, the enemy of our souls is utterly cut off!!

EXODUS

5:1: And afterward Moses and Aaron went in, and told Pharaoh, Thus saith the LORD God of Israel, Let my people go, that they may hold a **feast** unto me in the wilderness.

12:14: And this day shall be unto you for a memorial; and ye shall keep it a feast to the LORD throughout your generations; ye shall keep it a **feast** by an ordinance forever.

23:14: Three times, thou shalt keep a **feast** unto me in the year.

LEVITICUS

23:39: Also in the fifteenth day of the seventh month, when ye have gathered in the fruit of the land, ye shall **keep** a feast unto the LORD seven days: on the first day shall be a Sabbath, and on the eighth day shall be a Sabbath.

23:41: And ye shall **keep** it a feast unto the LORD seven days in the year. It shall be a statute forever in your generations: ye shall celebrate it in the seventh month.

NUMBERS

29:12: And on the fifteenth day of the seventh month, ye shall have an holy convocation; ye shall do no servile work, and ye shall keep a **feast** unto the LORD seven days:

DEUTERONOMY

16:15: Seven days shalt thou **keep a solemn feast** unto the LORD thy God in the place which the LORD shall choose: because the LORD thy God shall bless thee in all thine increase, and in all the works of thine hands, therefore thou shalt surely rejoice.

I SAMUEL

30:16: And when he had brought him down, behold, they were spread abroad upon all the earth, eating and drinking, and **dancing**, because of all the great spoil that they had taken out of the land of the Philistines, and out of the land of Judah.

PSALMS

42:4: When I remember these things, I pour out my soul in me: for I had gone with the multitude, I went with them to the house of God, with the voice of joy and praise, with a multitude that **kept holyday.**

NAHUM

1:15: Behold upon the mountains the feet of him that bringeth good tidings that publisheth peace! O Judah, **keep** thy solemn feasts, perform thy vows: for the wicked shall no more pass through thee; he is utterly cut off.

CHUL, CHUWL, CHIL

CHUL, CHUWL, OR CHIL – (Anguish; Pain; Travail; Troubled) *To twist or whirl in a circular or spiral manner; to dance; to turn around; to dance in a circle; also to writhe in pain (as in childbirth); to bring forth; to travail; to be born. This is said to be one of the only words associated with movement and intercession.*

DEUTERONOMY

2:25: This day will I begin to put the dread of thee and the fear of thee upon the nations that are under the whole heaven, who shall hear report of thee, and shall tremble, and be in **anguish** because of thee.

JOB

15:20: The wicked man **travaileth** with pain all his days, and the number of years is hidden to the oppressor.

PSALMS

55:4: My heart is sore **pained** within me: and the terrors of death are fallen upon me.

77:16: The waters saw thee, O God, the waters saw thee; they were afraid: the depths also were **troubled**.

ISAIAH

23:4: Be thou ashamed, O Zidon: for the sea hath spoken, even the strength of the sea, saying, I **travail** not, nor bring forth children, neither do I nourish up young men, nor bring up virgins.

23:5: As at the report concerning Egypt, so shall they be sorely **pained** at the report of Tyre.

26:17: Like as a woman with child, that draweth near the time of her delivery, is in **pain,** and crieth out in her pangs; so have we been in thy sight, O LORD.

26:18: We have been with child, we have been in **pain**, we have as it were brought forth wind; we have not wrought any deliverance in the earth; neither have the inhabitants of the world fallen.

54:1: Sing, O barren, thou that didst not bear; break forth into singing, and cry aloud, thou that didst not **travail** with child: for more are the children of the desolate than the children of the married wife, saith the LORD.

66:7: Before she **travailed**, she brought forth; before her pain came, she was delivered of a man-child.

66:8: Who hath heard such a thing? Who hath seen such things? Shall the earth be made to bring forth in one day? Or shall a nation be born at once? For as soon as Zion **travailed**, she brought forth her children.

JEREMIAH

4:19: My bowels, my bowels! I am **pained** at my very heart; my heart maketh a noise in me; I cannot hold my peace, because thou hast heard, O my soul, the sound of the trumpet, the alarm of war.

30:23: Behold, the whirlwind of the LORD goeth forth with fury, a continuing whirlwind: it shall fall with **pain** upon the head of the wicked.

EZEKIEL

30:16: And I will set fire in Egypt: Sin shall have **great pain**, and No shall be rent asunder, and Noph shall have distresses daily.

JOEL

2:6: Before their face the people shall be much **pained**: all faces shall gather blackness.

DALAG

DALAG – **(Leap)** *To spring or leap; Leap over.*

II SAMUEL

22:30: For by thee I have run through a troop: by my God have I **leaped** over a wall.

PSALMS

18:29: For by thee I have run through a troop; and by my God have I **leaped** over a wall.

SONG OF SOLOMON

2:8: The voice of my beloved! Behold, he cometh **leaping** upon the mountains, skipping upon the hills.

ISAIAH

35:6: Then shall the lame man **leap** as an hart, and the tongue of the dumb sing: for in the wilderness shall waters break out, and streams in the desert.

ZEPHANIAH

1:9: In the same day also will I punish all those that **leap** on the threshold, which fill their masters' houses with violence and deceit.

EALATS, EALAZ

EALATS OR EALAZ – (Triumph; Joyful; Rejoice)
To jump for joy; exult [root: salient—jumping; leaping; gushing or jetting forth; standing out from the rest; noticeable; conspicuous; prominent; the part of a battle line, trench, fort, etc., which projects farthest toward the enemy (to rejoice greatly; be jubilant; glory; to leap up; leap for joy; triumphant)].

I CHRONICLES

16:32: Let the sea roar, and the fullness thereof: let the fields **rejoice**, and all that is therein.

PSALMS

5:11: But let all those that put their trust in thee rejoice: let them ever shout for joy, because thou defendest them: let them also that love thy name be **joyful** in thee.

25:2: O my God, I trust in thee: let me not be ashamed, let not mine enemies **triumph** over me.

28:7: The LORD is my strength and my shield; my heart trusted in him, and I am helped: therefore, my heart greatly **rejoiceth**; and with my song will I praise him.

68:4: Sing unto God, sing praises to his name: extol him that rideth upon the heavens by his name JAH, and **rejoice** before him.

96:12: Let the field be joyful, and all that is therein: then shall all the trees of the wood **rejoice.**

PROVERBS

11:10: When it goeth well with the righteous, the city **rejoiceth**: and when the wicked perish, there is shouting.

GIL, GIYL, GUL, GUWL

GIL, GIYL, GUL, OR GUWL (Pronounced gool or geel) - (Rejoice; Be Joyful; Joy; Glad; Delight) *To spin around under the influence of any violent emotion (usually of joy or rejoicing); to go in a circle; to be glad; joy; be joyful; rejoice; cry out; exalt.*

I CHRONICLES

16:31: Let the heavens be glad, and let the earth **rejoice**: and let men say among the nations, The LORD reigneth.

PSALMS

2:11: Serve the LORD with fear, and **rejoice** with trembling.

9:14: That I may shew forth all thy praise in the gates of the daughter of Zion: I will **rejoice** in thy salvation.

13:4: Lest mine enemy say, I have prevailed against him; and those that trouble me **rejoice** when I am moved.

13:5: But I have trusted in thy mercy; my heart shall **rejoice** in thy salvation.

14:7: Oh that the salvation of Israel were come out of Zion! When the LORD bringeth back the captivity of his people, Jacob shall **rejoice**, and Israel shall be glad.

16:9: Therefore, my heart is glad, and my glory **rejoiceth**: my flesh also shall rest in hope.

21:1: The king shall joy in thy strength, O LORD; and in thy salvation how greatly shall he **rejoice**!

31:7: I will **be glad** and rejoice in thy mercy: for thou hast considered my trouble; thou hast known my soul in adversities;

32:11: Be glad in the LORD, and **rejoice**, ye righteous: and shout for joy, all ye that are upright in heart.

35:9: And my soul shall **be joyful** in the LORD: it shall rejoice in his salvation.

48:11: Let mount Zion rejoice, let the daughters of Judah **be glad,** because of thy judgments.

51:8: Make me to hear joy and gladness; that the bones,which thou hast broken, may **rejoice**.

53:6: Oh that the salvation of Israel were come out of Zion! When God bringeth back the captivity of his people, Jacob shall **rejoice**, and Israel shall be glad.

89:16: In thy name shall they **rejoice** all the day: and in thy righteousness shall they be exalted.

96:11: Let the heavens rejoice, and let the earth **be glad;** let the sea roar, and the fullness thereof.

97:1: The LORD reigneth; let the earth **rejoice**; let the multitude of isles be glad thereof.

97:8: Zion heard, and was glad; and the daughters of Judah **rejoiced** because of thy judgments, O LORD.

118:24: This is the day, which the LORD hath made; we will **rejoice** and be glad in it.

149:2: Let Israel rejoice in him that made him: let the children of Zion **be joyful** in their King.

PROVERBS

2:14: Who rejoice to do evil, and **delight** in the forwardness of the wicked;

23:24: The father of the righteous shall greatly **rejoice**: and he that begetteth a wise child shall have joy of him.

23:25: Thy father and thy mother shall be glad, and she that bare thee shall **rejoice**.

24:17: Rejoice not when thine enemy falleth, and let not thine heart **be glad** when he stumbleth:

SONG OF SOLOMON

1:4: Draw me, we will run after thee: the king hath brought me into his chambers: we will **be glad** and rejoice in thee, we will remember thy love more than wine: the upright loves thee.

ISAIAH

9:3: Thou hast multiplied the nation, and not increased the joy: they joy before thee according to the joy in harvest, and as men **rejoice** when they divide the spoil.

25:9: And it shall be said in that day, Lo, this is our God; we have waited for him, and he will save us: this is the LORD; we have waited for him, we will **be glad** and rejoice in his salvation.

29:19: The meek also shall increase their joy in the LORD, and the poor among men shall **rejoice** in the Holy One of Israel.

35:1: The wilderness and the solitary place shall be glad for them; and the desert shall **rejoice**, and blossom as the rose.

35:2: It shall blossom abundantly, and **rejoice** even with joy and singing: the glory of Lebanon shall be given unto it, the Excellency of Carmel and Sharon, they shall see the glory of the LORD, and the Excellency of our God.

41:16: Thou shalt fan them, the wind shall carry them away, and the whirlwind shall scatter them: and thou shalt **rejoice** in the LORD, and shalt glory in the Holy One of Israel.

49:13: Sing, O heavens; and **be joyful**, O earth; and break forth into singing, O mountains: for the LORD hath comforted his people, and will have mercy upon his afflicted.

65:18: But be ye glad and **rejoice** forever in that which I create: for, behold, I create Jerusalem a rejoicing, and her people a joy.

65:19: And I will **rejoice** in Jerusalem, and joy in my people: and the voice of weeping shall be no more heard in her, nor the voice of crying.

66:10: Rejoice ye with Jerusalem, and **be glad** with her, all ye that love her: rejoice for joy with her, all ye that mourn for her:

HOSEA

10:5: The inhabitants of Samaria shall fear because of the calves of Beth-aven: for the people thereof shall mourn over it, and the priests thereof that **rejoiced** on it, for the glory thereof, because it is departed from it.

JOEL

2:21: Fear not, O land; **be glad** and rejoice: for the LORD will do great things.

2:23: Be glad then, ye children of Zion, and rejoice in the LORD your God: for he hath given you the former rain moderately, and he will cause to come down for you the rain, the former rain, and the latter rain in the first month.

HABAKKUK

1:15: They take up all of them with the angle, they catch them in their net, and gather them in their drag: therefore, they rejoice and are **glad.**

3:18: Yet I will rejoice in the LORD, I will **joy** in the God of my salvation.

ZEPHANIAH

3:17: The LORD thy God in the midst of thee is mighty; he will save, he will rejoice over thee with joy; he will rest in his love, he will **joy** over thee with singing.

ZECHARIAH

9:9: Rejoice greatly, O daughter of Zion; shout, O daughter of Jerusalem: behold, thy King cometh unto thee: he is just, and having salvation; lowly, and riding upon an ass, and upon a colt the foal of an ass.

10:7: And they of Ephraim shall be like a mighty man, and their heart shall rejoice as through wine: yea, their children shall see it, and be glad; their heart shall **rejoice** in the LORD.

HALAL

HALAL – (Praise; Celebrate) *To be clear; to shine; to make a show; to spin around; to rave; to boast, and thus to be clamorously foolish; glory; give in marriage; praise; rage; renowned; to celebrate. This is the root word for Hallelujah, and is the most basic and widely used word for praise in the Old Testament.*

I CHRONICLES

16:4: And he appointed certain of the Levites to minister before the ark of the LORD, and to record, and to thank and **praise** the LORD God of Israel:

23:5: Moreover, four thousand were porters; and four thousand praised the LORD with the instruments, which I made, said David, to **praise** therewith.

23:30: And to stand every morning to thank and **praise** the LORD, and likewise at even;

25:3: Of Jeduthun: the sons of Jeduthun; Gedaliah, and Zeri, and Jeshaiah, Hashabiah, and Mattithiah, six, under the hands of their father Jeduthun, who prophesied with a harp, to give thanks and to **praise** the LORD.

29:13: Now therefore, our God, we thank thee, and **praise** thy glorious name.

II CHRONICLES

5:13: It came even to pass, as the trumpeters and singers were as one, to make one sound to be heard in **praising** and thanking the LORD; and when they lifted up their voice with the trumpets and cymbals and instruments of musick, and praised the LORD, saying, For he is good; for his mercy endureth for ever: that then the house was filled with a cloud, even the house of the LORD;

7:6: And the priests waited on their offices: the Levites also with instruments of musick of the LORD, which David the king had made to praise the LORD, because his mercy endureth for ever, when David **praised** by their ministry; and the priests sounded trumpets before them, and all Israel stood.

8:14: And he appointed, according to the order of David his father, the courses of the priests to their service, and the Levites to their charges, to **praise** and minister before the priests, as the duty of every day required: the porters also by their courses at every gate: for so had David the man of God commanded.

20:19: And the Levites, of the children of the Kohathites, and of the children of the Korhites, stood up to **praise** the LORD God of Israel with a loud voice on high.

23:12: Now when Athaliah heard the noise of the people running and **praising** the king, she came to the people into the house of the LORD:

23:13: And she looked, and, behold, the king stood at his pillar at the entering in, and the princes and the trumpets by the king: and all the people of the land rejoiced, and sounded with trumpets, also the singers with instruments of musick, and such as taught to sing **praise**. Then Athaliah rent her clothes, and said, Treason, Treason.

31:2: And Hezekiah appointed the courses of the priests and the Levites after their courses, every man according to his service, the priests and Levites for burnt offerings and for peace offerings, to minister, and to give thanks, and to **praise** in the gates of the tents of the LORD.

EZRA

3:10: And when the builders laid the foundation of the temple of the LORD, they set the priests in their apparel with trumpets, and the Levites the sons of Asaph with cymbals, to **praise** the LORD, after the ordinance of David king of Israel.

3:11: And they sang together by course in **praising** and giving thanks unto the LORD; because he is good, for his mercy endureth for ever toward Israel. And all the people shouted with a great shout, when they **praised** the LORD, because the foundation of the house of the LORD was laid.

NEHEMIAH

12:24: And the chief of the Levites: Hashabiah, Sherebiah, and Jeshua the son of Kadmiel, with their brethren over against them, to **praise** and to give thanks, according to the commandment of David the man of God, ward over against ward.

PSALMS

22:22: I will declare thy name unto my brethren: in the midst of the congregation will I **praise** thee.

22:23: Ye that fear the LORD, **praise** him; all ye the seed of Jacob, glorify him; and fear him, all ye the seed of Israel.

22:26: The meek shall eat and be satisfied: they shall **praise** the LORD that seeks him: your heart shall live forever.

35:18: I will give thee thanks in the great congregation: I will **praise** thee among much people.

56:4: In God I will **praise** his word, in God I have put my trust; I will not fear what flesh can do unto me.

63:5: My soul shall be satisfied as with marrow and fatness; and my mouth shall **praise** thee with joyful lips:

69:30: I will **praise** the name of God with a song, and will magnify him with thanksgiving.

74:21: O let not the oppressed return ashamed: let the poor and needy **praise** thy name.

84:4: Blessed are they that dwell in thy house: they will be still **praising** thee. Selah.

102:18: This shall be written for the generation to come: and the people who shall be created shall **praise** the LORD.

104:35: Let the sinners be consumed out of the earth, and let the wicked be no more. Bless thou the LORD, O my soul. **Praise** ye the LORD.

105:45: That they might observe his statutes, and keep his laws. **Praise** ye the LORD.

106:1: Praise ye the LORD. O give thanks unto the LORD; for he is good: for his mercy endureth for ever.

107:32: Let them exalt him also in the congregation of the people, and **praise** him in the assembly of the elders.

109:30: I will greatly praise the LORD with my mouth; yea, I will **praise** him among the multitude.

111:1: Praise ye the LORD. I will praise the LORD with my whole heart, in the assembly of the upright, and in the congregation.

112:1: Praise ye the LORD. Blessed is the man that feareth the LORD that delighteth greatly in his commandments.

113:1: Praise ye the LORD. **Praise,** O ye servants of the LORD, **praise** the name of the LORD.

113:9: He maketh the barren woman to keep house, and to be a joyful mother of children. **Praise** ye the LORD.

115:17: The dead **praise** not the LORD, neither any that go down into silence.

115:18: But we will bless the LORD from this time forth and for evermore. **Praise** the LORD.

116:19: In the courts of the LORD'S house, in the midst of thee, O Jerusalem. **Praise** ye the LORD.

117:1: O **praise** the LORD, all ye nations: praise him, all ye people.

117:2: For his merciful kindness is great toward us: and the truth of the LORD endureth forever. **Praise** ye the LORD.

119:164: Seven times a day do I **praise** thee because of thy righteous judgments.

119:175: Let my soul live, and it shall **praise** thee; and let thy judgments help me.

135:1: Praise ye the LORD. Praise ye the name of the LORD; praise him, O ye servants of the LORD.

135:3: Praise the LORD; for the LORD is good: sing praises unto his name; for it is pleasant.

135:21: Blessed be the LORD out of Zion, which dwelleth at Jerusalem. **Praise** ye the LORD.

145:2: Every day will I bless thee; and I will **praise** thy name for ever and ever.

145:3: Great is the LORD, and greatly to be **praised**; and his greatness is unsearchable.

146:1: Praise ye the LORD. **Praise** the LORD, O my soul.

146:2: While I live will I **praise** the LORD: I will sing praises unto my God while I have any being.

146:10: The LORD shall reign for ever, even thy God, O Zion, unto all generations. **Praise** ye the LORD.

147:1: Praise ye the LORD: for it is good to sing praises unto our God; for it is pleasant; and praise is comely.

147:12: Praise the LORD, O Jerusalem; **praise** thy God, O Zion.

147:20: He hath not dealt so with any nation: and as for his judgments, they have not known them. **Praise** ye the LORD.

148:1: Praise ye the LORD. **Praise** ye the LORD from the heavens: **praise** him in the heights.

148:2: Praise ye him, all his angels: **praise** ye him, all his hosts.

148:3: Praise ye him, sun and moon: **praise** him, all ye stars of light.

148:4: Praise him, ye heavens of heavens, and ye waters that be above the heavens.

148:5: Let them **praise** the name of the LORD: for he commanded, and they were created.

148:7: Praise the LORD from the earth, ye dragons, and all deeps:

149:1: Praise ye the LORD. Sing unto the LORD a new song, and his praise in the congregation of saints.

150:1: Praise ye the LORD. **Praise** God in his sanctuary: **praise** him in the firmament of his power.

150:2: Praise him for his mighty acts: **praise** him according to his excellent greatness.

150:3: Praise him with the sound of the trumpet: **praise** him with the psaltery and harp.

150:4: Praise him with the timbrel and dance: **praise** him with stringed instruments and organs.

150:5: Praise him upon the loud cymbals: **praise** him upon the high sounding cymbals.

150:6: Let every thing that hath breath **praise** the LORD. Praise ye the LORD.

PROVERBS

31:31: Give her of the fruit of her hands; and let her own works **praise** her in the gates.

ISAIAH

38:18: For the grave cannot praise thee, death cannot **celebrate** thee: they that go down into the pit cannot hope for thy truth.

62:9: But they that have gathered it shall eat it, and **praise** the LORD; and they that have brought it together shall drink it in the courts of my holiness.

JEREMIAH

31:7: For thus saith the LORD; Sing with gladness for Jacob, and shout among the chief of the nations: publish ye, **praise** ye, and say, O LORD, save thy people, the remnant of Israel.

JOEL

2:26: And ye shall eat in plenty, and be satisfied, and **praise** the name of the LORD your God that hath dealt wondrously with you: and my people shall never be ashamed.

HALIYKAH, HALIJKAH

HALIYKAH OR HALIJKAH – **(Ways; Companies; Goings)** *walking, moving or marching in a procession, caravan, or traveling company; a march; a going; way.*

JOB

6:19: The troops of Tema looked, the **companies** of Sheba waited for them.

PSALMS

68:24: They have seen thy **goings**, O God; even the **goings** of my God, my King, in the sanctuary.

PROVERBS

31:27: She looketh well to the **ways** of her household, and eateth not the bread of idleness.

NAHUM

2:5: He shall recount his worthies: they shall stumble in their **walk**; they shall make hast to the wall thereof, and the defense shall be prepared.

HABAKKUK

3:6: He stood, and measured the earth: he beheld, and drove asunder the nations; and the everlasting mountains were scattered, the perpetual hills did bow: his **ways** are everlasting.

KARAR

KARAR – (Danced; Dancing); *dancing; to go around in a circle; to dance or whirl; to leap, exult, run. On an interesting side note, the word 'KAR' is a derivative from the primitive root Karar and means battering ram. Combined with Karar, which means to whirl, this type of dance could mean a battering ram that whirls against the enemy – what a powerful depiction!*

II SAMUEL

6:14: And David **danced** before the LORD with all his might; and David was girded with a linen ephod.

6:16: And as the ark of the LORD came into the city of David, Michal Saul's daughter looked through a window, and saw king David leaping and **dancing** before the LORD; and she despised him in her heart.

MACHOWL, MACHOL

MACHOWL OR MACHOL – **(Dance)** *A round dance; dancing; chorus.*

PSALMS

30:11: Thou hast turned for me my mourning into **dancing**: thou hast put off my sackcloth, and girded me with gladness.

149:3: Let them praise his name in the **dance**: let them sing praises unto him with the timbrel and harp.

150:4: Praise him with the timbrel and **dance**: praise him with stringed instruments and organs.

LAMENTATIONS

5:15: The joy of our heart is ceased; our **dance** is turned into mourning.

**MACHOLAH OR MECHOWLAH – (Dance; Compa-
ny)** *A dance; a dance company or chorus; dances (fem.
of Machowl).*

EXODUS

15:20: And Miriam the prophetess, the sister of Aaron, took a timbrel in her hand; and all the women went out after her with timbrels and with **dances**.

32:19: And it came to pass, as soon as he came nigh unto the camp, that he saw the calf, and the **dancing**: and Moses' anger waxed hot, and he cast the tables out of his hands, and brake them beneath the mount.

JUDGES

11:34: And Jephthah came to Mizpeh unto his house, and, behold, his daughter came out to meet him with timbrels and with **dances**: and she was his only child; beside her he had neither son nor daughter.

21:21: And see, and, behold, if the daughters of Shiloh come out to dance in **dances**, then come ye out of the vineyards, and catch you every man his wife of the daughters of Shiloh, and go to the land of Benjamin.

I SAMUEL

18:6: And it came to pass as they came, when David was returned from the slaughter of the Philistine, that the women came out of all cities of Israel, singing and **dancing**, to meet king Saul, with tabrets, with joy, and with instruments of musick.

21:11: And the servants of Achish said unto him, Is not this David the king of the land? did they not sing one to another of him in **dances**, saying, Saul hath slain his thousands, and David his ten thousands?

29:5: Is not this David, of whom they sang one to another in **dances**, saying, Saul slew his thousands, and David his ten thousands?

SONG OF SOLOMON

6:13: Return, return, O Shulamite; return, return, that we may look upon thee. What will ye see in the Shulamite? As it were, the **company** of two armies.

NATHAR

NATHAR – (Undo; Make; Loose) *To jump; to shake off; untie; to terrify. The Lord wants us to be free. Through the movement of shaking off and the type of fast He calls, He will bring deliverance, thus indicating that dancing (which terrifies the enemy) causes a loosening or shaking off of bondage.*

II SAMUEL

22:33: God is my strength and power: and he **maketh** my way perfect.

PSALMS

146:7: Which executeth judgment for the oppressed: which giveth food to the hungry. The LORD **looseth** the prisoners.

ISAIAH

58:6: Is not this the fast that I have chosen? to loose the bands of wickedness, **to undo** the heavy burdens, and to let the oppressed go free, and that ye break every yoke?

PAZAZ

PAZAZ – (Made Strong; Leaping) *To spring as if separating the limbs, like leaping; to bound; to be light and agile; to be made strong; to solidify, as if by refining*

GENESIS

49:24: But his bow abode in strength, and the arms of his hands were **made strong** by the hands of the mighty God of Jacob; (from thence is the shepherd, the stone of Israel:)

II SAMUEL

6:16: And as the ark of the LORD came into the city of David, Michal Saul's daughter looked through a window, and saw king David **leaping** and dancing before the LORD; and she despised him in her heart.

RAQAD, REKAD

RAQAD OR REKAD – (Dance; Skip; Leap; Jump; Worship) *To stamp; spring about wildly for joy; dance; jump; leap; skip.*

I CHRONICLES

15:29: And it came to pass, as the ark of the covenant of the LORD came to the city of David, that Michal the daughter of Saul looking out at a window saw king David **dancing** and playing: and she despised him in her heart.

JOB

21:11: They send forth their little ones like a flock, and their children **dance**.

PSALMS

29:6: He maketh them also to **skip** like a calf; Lebanon and Sirion like a young unicorn.

114:4: The mountains **skipped** like rams, and the little hills like lambs.

114:6: Ye mountains, that ye **skipped** like rams; and ye little hills, like lambs?

ECCLESIASTES

3:4: A time to weep, and a time to laugh; a time to mourn, and a time to **dance**.

ISAIAH

13:21: But wild beasts of the desert shall lie there; and their houses shall be full of doleful creatures; and owls shall dwell there, and satyrs shall **dance** there.

JOEL

2:5: Like the noise of chariots on the tops of mountains shall they **leap**, like the noise of a flame of fire that devoureth the stubble, as a strong people set in battle array.

NAHUM

3:2: The noise of a whip, and the noise of the rattling of the wheels, and of the praising horses, and of the **jumping** chariots.

SHACHAH

SHACHAH – (Worship) *To depress; press down; to prostrate in homage to royalty or worship of God.*

EXODUS

33:10: And all the people saw the cloudy pillar stand at the tabernacle door: and all the people rose up and **worshipped** every man in his tent door.

DUETERONOMY

26:10: And now, behold, I have brought the first fruits of the land, which thou, O LORD, hast given me. And thou shalt set it before the LORD thy God, and **worship** before the LORD thy God:

I CHRONICLES

16:29: Give unto the LORD the glory due unto his name: bring an offering, and come before him: **worship** the LORD in the beauty of holiness.

II CHRONICLES

20:18: And Jehoshaphat bowed his head with his face to the ground: and all Judah and the inhabitants of Jerusalem fell before the LORD, **worshipping** the LORD.

PSALMS

29:2: Give unto the LORD the glory due unto his name; **worship** the LORD in the beauty of holiness.

96:9: O **worship** the LORD in the beauty of holiness: fear before him, all the earth.

99:5: Exalt ye the LORD our God, and **worship** at his footstool; for he is holy.

99:9: Exalt the LORD our God, and **worship** at his holy hill; for the LORD our God is holy.

SHIYR

SHIYR – (Sing; Singer) – *Strolling along with song; travel; to turn; song leaders; singers; to sing; as a strolling minstrel.*

EXODUS

15:1: Then sang Moses and the children of Israel this song unto the LORD, and spake, saying, I will **sing** unto the LORD, for he hath triumphed gloriously: the horse and his rider hath he thrown into the sea.

15:21: And Miriam answered them, **Sing** ye to the LORD, for he hath triumphed gloriously; the horse and his rider hath he thrown into the sea.

JUDGES

5:3: Hear, O ye kings; give ear, O ye princes; I, even I, will **sing** unto the LORD; I will sing praise to the LORD God of Israel.

I KINGS

10:12: And the king made of the almug trees pillars for the house of the LORD, and for the king's house, harps also and psalteries for **singers**: there came no such almug trees, nor were seen unto this day.

I CHRONICLES

6:33: And these are they that waited with their children. Of the sons of the Kohathites: Heman a **singer**, the son of Joel, the son of Shemuel

9:33: And these are the **singers**, chief of the fathers of the Levites, who remaining in the chambers were free: for they were employed in that work day and night.

16:9: Sing unto him, sing psalms unto him, talk ye of all his wondrous works.

16:23: Sing unto the LORD, all the earth; shew forth from day to day his salvation.

PSALMS

13:6: I will **sing** unto the LORD, because he hath dealt bountifully with me.

21:13: Be thou exalted, LORD, in thine own strength: so will we **sing** and praise thy power.

27:6: And now shall mine head be lifted up above mine enemies round about me: therefore will I offer in his tabernacle sacrifices of joy; I will **sing**, yea, I will sing praises unto the LORD.

33:3: Sing unto him a new song; play skilfully with a loud noise.

57:7: My heart is fixed, O God, my heart is fixed: I will **sing** and give praise.

59:16: But I will **sing** of thy power; yea, I will sing aloud of thy mercy in the morning: for thou hast been my defense and refuge in the day of my trouble.

65:13: The pastures are clothed with flocks; the valleys also are covered over with corn; they shout for joy, they also **sing**.

68:4: Sing unto God, sing praises to his name: extol him that rideth upon the heavens by his name JAH, and rejoice before him.

68:32: Sing unto God, ye kingdoms of the earth; O sing praises unto the Lord; Selah:

87:7: As well the **singers** as the players on instruments shall be there: all my springs are in thee.

89:1: I will **sing** of the mercies of the LORD for ever: with my mouth will I make known thy faithfulness to all generations.

96:1: O **sing** unto the LORD a new song: **sing** unto the LORD, all the earth.

96:2: Sing unto the LORD, bless his name; shew forth his salvation from day to day.

98:1: O **sing** unto the LORD a new song; for he hath done marvelous things: his right hand, and his holy arm, hath gotten him the victory.

101:1: I will **sing** of mercy and judgment: unto thee, O LORD, will I sing.

104:33: I will **sing** unto the LORD as long as I live: I will sing praise to my God while I have my being.

105:2: Sing unto him, sing psalms unto him: talk ye of all his wondrous works.

108:1: O God, my heart is fixed; I will **sing** and give praise, even with my glory.

137:3: For there they that carried us away captive required of us a song; and they that wasted us required of us mirth, saying, **Sing** us one of the songs of Zion.

137:4: How shall we **sing** the LORD'S song in a strange land?

138:5: Yea, they shall **sing** in the ways of the LORD: for great is the glory of the LORD.

144:9: I will **sing** a new song unto thee, O God: upon a psaltery and an instrument of ten strings will I sing praises unto thee.

149:1: Praise ye the LORD. **Sing** unto the LORD a new song, and his praise in the congregation of saints.

ISAIAH

5:1: Now will I **sing** to my well beloved a song of my beloved touching his vineyard. My well beloved hath a vineyard in a very fruitful hill:

42:10: Sing unto the LORD a new song, and his praise from the end of the earth, ye that go down to the sea, and all that is therein; the isles, and the inhabitants thereof.

JEREMIAH

20:13: Sing unto the LORD, praise ye the LORD: for he hath delivered the soul of the poor from the hand of evildoers.

ZEPHANIAH

2:14: And flocks shall lie down in the midst of her, all the beasts of the nations: both the cormorant and the bittern shall lodge in the upper lintels of it; their voice shall **sing** in the windows; desolation shall be in the thresholds: for he shall uncover the cedar work.

TNUWPHAH

TNUWPHAH combined with primitive root NUW-PH (Wave; Wave Offering; Move; Lift Up; Strike)– *A brandishing (threat) tumult; wars of shaking; tumultuous wars; the undulation of sacrificial offerings; offering; shaking; shaking of the hand, as a gesture of threatening; wave; to move to and fro; to swing, wield, brandish against; to be waved; of God's hand, weapons; of sacrifices before Jehovah; a particular rite in offering; as a perfume of fire that drives out the occupant (enemy).*

EXODUS

29:24 And thou shalt put all in the hands of Aaron, and in the hands of his sons; and shalt **wave** them [for] a **wave offering** before the LORD.

29:26 And thou shalt take the breast of the ram of Aaron's consecration, and **wave** it [for] a **wave offering** before the LORD: and it shall be thy part.

29:27 And thou shalt sanctify the breast of the **wave offering,** and the shoulder of the heave **offering,** which is **waved,** and which is heaved up, of the ram of the consecration, [even] of [that] which [is] for Aaron, and of [that] which is for his sons:

LEVITICUS

7:30 His own hands shall bring the offerings of the LORD made by fire, the fat with the breast, it shall he bring, that the breast may be **waved** [for] a **wave offering** before the LORD.

7:34 For the **wave** breast and the heave shoulder have I taken of the children of Israel from off the sacrifices of their peace offerings, and have given them unto Aaron the priest and unto his sons by a statute for ever from among the children of Israel.

8:27 And he put all upon Aaron's hands, and upon his sons' hands, and **waved** them [for] a **wave offering** before the LORD.

8:29 And Moses took the breast, and **waved** it [for] a **wave offering** before the LORD: [for] of the ram of consecration it was Moses' part; as the LORD commanded Moses.

9:21 And the breasts and the right shoulder Aaron **waved** [for] a **wave offering** before the LORD; as Moses commanded.

10:14 And the **wave** breast and heave shoulder shall ye eat in a clean place; thou, and thy sons, and thy daughters with thee: for [they be] thy due, and thy sons' due, [which] are given out of the sacrifices of peace offerings of the children of Israel.

10:15 The heave shoulder and the **wave** breast shall they bring with the offerings made by fire of the fat, to **wave** [it for] a **wave offering** before the LORD; and it shall be thine, and thy sons' with thee, by a statute for ever; as the LORD hath commanded.

14:12 And the priest shall take one he lamb, and offer him for a trespass offering, and the log of oil, and **wave** them [for] a **wave offering** before the LORD:

14:24 And the priest shall take the lamb of the trespass **offering,** and the log of oil, and the priest shall **wave** them [for] a **wave offering** before the LORD:

23:11 And he shall **wave** the sheaf before the LORD, to be accepted for you: on the morrow after the sabbath the priest shall **wave** it.

23:12 And ye shall offer that day when ye **wave** the sheaf an he lamb without blemish of the first year for a burnt offering unto the LORD.

23:15 And ye shall count unto you from the morrow after the sabbath, from the day that ye brought the sheaf of the **wave offering;** seven sabbaths shall be complete:

23:17 Ye shall bring out of your habitations two **wave** loaves of two tenth deals: they shall be of fine flour; they shall be baken with leaven; [they are] the first-fruits unto the LORD.

23:20 And the priest shall **wave** them with the bread of the firstfruits [for] a **wave offering** before the LORD, with the two lambs: they shall be holy to the LORD for the priest.

NUMBERS

5:25 Then the priest shall take the jealousy offering out of the woman's hand, and shall **wave** the offering before the LORD, and offer it upon the altar:

6:20 And the priest shall **wave** them [for] a **wave offering** before the LORD: this [is] holy for the priest, with the **wave** breast and heave shoulder: and after that the Nazarite may drink wine.

18:11 And this [is] thine; the heave offering of their gift, with all the **wave offerings** of the children of Israel: I have given them unto thee, and to thy sons and to thy daughters with thee, by a statute for ever: every one that is clean in thy house shall eat of it.

18:18 And the flesh of them shall be thine, as the **wave** breast and as the right shoulder are thine.

DEUTERONOMY

23:25 When thou comest into the standing corn of thy neighbour, then thou mayest pluck the ears with thine hand; but thou shalt not **move** a sickle unto thy neighbour's standing corn.

27:5 And there shalt thou build an altar unto the LORD thy God, an altar of stones: thou shalt not **lift up** [any] iron [tool] upon them.

JOSHUA

8:31 As Moses the servant of the LORD commanded the children of Israel, as it is written in the book of the law of Moses, an altar of whole stones, over which no man hath **lift up** [any] iron: and they offered thereon burnt offerings unto the LORD, and sacrificed peace offerings.

2 KINGS

5:11 But Naaman was wroth, and went away, and said, Behold, I thought, He will surely come out to me, and stand, and call on the name of the LORD his God, and **strike** his hand over the place, and recover the leper.

TOWDAH

TOWDAH – (Praise; Thanksgiving) *Comes from the root word Yadah (which means to praise the Lord with extended hand and graceful gestures). However, Todah indicates plurality or a lot of hands extending to praise and worship God through movement. It also indicates a sacrifice of praise in adoration and thanks; a choir of worshippers; avowal (open acknowledgment or declaration; frank admission).*

II CHRONICLES

29:31: Then Hezekiah answered and said, Now ye have consecrated yourselves unto the LORD, come near and bring sacrifices and thank offerings into the house of the LORD. And the congregation brought in sacrifices and **thank offerings**; and as many as were of a free heart burnt offerings.

PSALMS

26:7: That I may publish with the voice of **thanksgiving**, and tell of all thy wondrous works.

42:4: When I remember these things, I pour out my soul in me: for I had gone with the multitude, I went with them to the house of God, with the voice of joy and **praise**, with a multitude that kept holy day.

50:14: Offer unto God **thanksgiving**; and pay thy vows unto the most High.

50:23: Whoso offereth **praise** glorifieth me: and to him that ordereth his conversation aright will I shew the salvation of God.

56:12: Thy vows are upon me, O God: I will render **praises** unto thee.

95:2: Let us come before his presence with **thanksgiving**, and make a joyful noise unto him with psalms.

100:4: Enter into his gates with **thanksgiving**, and into his courts with praise: be thankful unto him, and bless his name.

107:22: And let them sacrifice the sacrifices of **thanksgiving**, and declare his works with rejoicing.

116:17: I will offer to thee the sacrifice of **thanksgiving**, and will call upon the name of the LORD.

JEREMIAH

17:26: And they shall come from the cities of Judah, and from the places about Jerusalem, and from the land of Benjamin, and from the plain, and from the mountains, and from the south, bringing burnt offerings, and sacrifices, and meat offerings, and incense, and bringing sacrifices of **praise**, unto the house of the LORD.

33:11: The voice of joy, and the voice of gladness, the voice of the bridegroom, and the voice of the bride, the voice of them that shall say, Praise the LORD of hosts: for the LORD is good; for his mercy endureth for ever: and of them that shall bring the sacrifice of **praise** into the house of the LORD. For I will cause to return the captivity of the land, as at the first, saith the LORD

YADAH

YADAH – (Praise; Thank) *To hold out or use the hand; to revere or worship with extended, flourishing (to make showy, wavy motions as of the arms; done in a showy way, as a sweeping movement of the limbs or body) hands; raising the hands with graceful gestures; glorify; give thanks; shout; praise; make confession; to cast out; to use the hands in a motion of throwing;*

GENESIS

29:35: And she conceived again, and bare a son: and she said, Now will I **praise** the LORD: therefore she called his name Judah; and left bearing.

49:8: Judah, thou art he whom thy brethren shall **praise**: thy hand shall be in the neck of thine enemies; thy father's children shall bow down before thee.

I CHRONICLES

16:4: And he appointed certain of the Levites to minister before the ark of the LORD, and to record, and **to thank** and praise the LORD God of Israel:

16:7: Then on that day David delivered first this psalm to **thank** the LORD into the hand of Asaph and his brethren.

16:35: And say ye, Save us, O God of our salvation, and gather us together, and deliver us from the heathen, that we may **give thanks** to thy holy name, and glory in thy praise.

16:41: And with them Heman and Jeduthun, and the rest that were chosen, who were expressed by name, to **give thanks** to the LORD, because his mercy endureth for ever;

II CHRONICLES

5:13: It came even to pass, as the trumpeters and singers were as one, to make one sound to be heard in praising and **thanking** the LORD; and when they lifted up their voice with the trumpets and cymbals and instruments of musick, and praised the LORD, saying, For he is good; for his mercy endureth for ever: that then the house was filled with a cloud, even the house of the LORD;

7:3: And when all the children of Israel saw how the fire came down, and the glory of the LORD upon the house, they bowed themselves with their faces to the ground upon the pavement, and worshipped, and **praised** the LORD, saying, For he is good; for his mercy endureth for ever.

7:6: And the priests waited on their offices: the Levites also with instruments of musick of the LORD, which David the king had made to **praise** the LORD, because his mercy endureth for ever, when David praised by their ministry; and the priests sounded trumpets before them, and all Israel stood.

20:21: And when he had consulted with the people, he appointed singers unto the LORD, and that should praise the beauty of holiness, as they went out before the army, and to say, **Praise** the LORD; for his mercy endureth for ever.

PSALMS

7:17: I will **praise** the LORD according to his righteousness: and will sing praise to the name of the LORD most high.

9:1: I will **praise** thee, O LORD, with my whole heart; I will shew forth all thy marvellous works.

28:7: The LORD is my strength and my shield; my heart trusted in him, and I am helped: therefore my heart greatly rejoiceth; and with my song will I **praise** him.

33:2: Praise the LORD with harp: sing unto him with the psaltery and an instrument of ten strings.

42:5: Why art thou cast down, O my soul? and why art thou disquieted in me? hope thou in God: for I shall yet **praise** him for the help of his countenance.

42:11: Why art thou cast down, O my soul? and why art thou disquieted within me? hope thou in God: for I shall yet **praise** him, who is the health of my countenance, and my God.

43:4: Then will I go unto the altar of God, unto God my exceeding joy: yea, upon the harp will I **praise** thee, O God my God.

43:5: Why art thou cast down, O my soul? and why art thou disquieted within me? hope in God: for I shall yet **praise** him, who is the health of my countenance, and my God.

44:8: In God we boast all the day long, and **praise** thy name for ever. Selah.

45:17: I will make thy name to be remembered in all generations: therefore shall the people **praise** thee for ever and ever.

49:18: Though while he lived he blessed his soul: and men will **praise** thee, when thou doest well to thyself.

52:9: I will **praise** thee for ever, because thou hast done it: and I will wait on thy name; for it is good before thy saints.

57:9: I will **praise** thee, O Lord, among the people: I will sing unto thee among the nations.

67:3: Let the people **praise** thee, O God; let all the people **praise** thee.

67:5: Let the people **praise** thee, O God; let all the people **praise** thee.

71:22: I will also **praise** thee with the psaltery, even thy truth, O my God: unto thee will I sing with the harp, O thou Holy One of Israel.

76:10: Surely the wrath of man shall **praise** thee: the remainder of wrath shalt thou restrain.

86:12: I will **praise** thee, O Lord my God, with all my heart: and I will glorify thy name for evermore.

88:10: Wilt thou shew wonders to the dead? shall the dead arise and **praise** thee? Selah.

89:5: And the heavens shall **praise** thy wonders, O LORD: thy faithfulness also in the congregation of the saints.

92:1: It is a good thing to **give thanks** unto the LORD, and to sing praises unto thy name, O most High:

99:3: Let them **praise** thy great and terrible name; for it is holy.

107:8: Oh that men would **praise** the LORD for his goodness, and for his wonderful works to the children of men!

108:3: I will **praise** thee, O LORD, among the people: and I will sing praises unto thee among the nations.

109:30: I will greatly **praise** the LORD with my mouth; yea, I will praise him among the multitude.

111:1: Praise ye the LORD. I will **praise** the LORD with my whole heart, in the assembly of the upright, and in the congregation.

118:19: Open to me the gates of righteousness: I will go into them, and I will **praise** the LORD:

ISAIAH

12:1: And in that day thou shalt say, O LORD, I will **praise** thee: though thou wast angry with me, thine anger is turned away, and thou comfortedst me.

25:1: O LORD, thou art my God; I will exalt thee, I will **praise** thy name; for thou hast done wonderful things; thy counsels of old are faithfulness and truth.

38:18: For the grave cannot **praise** thee, death can not celebrate thee: they that go down into the pit cannot hope for thy truth.

38:19: The living, the living, he shall **praise** thee, as I do this day: the father to the children shall make known thy truth.

JEREMIAH

33:11: The voice of joy, and the voice of gladness, the voice of the bridegroom, and the voice of the bride, the voice of them that shall say, **Praise** the LORD of hosts: for the LORD is good; for his mercy endureth for ever: and of them that shall bring the sacrifice of praise into the house of the LORD. For I will cause to return the captivity of the land, as at the first, saith the LORD.

DANCE PART III
New Testament Greek Words Pertaining to Dance or Movement

This section can be used exactly like Part II, except that the alphabetical listing is of the Greek words.

AGALLIASIS

AGALLIASIS – (Rejoice; Leap; Gladness; Joy)
Very much leaping; Jump for joy; exult; leap up; be exceedingly glad or joyful; to make glorious; exalt; rejoice greatly.

LUKE

1:14: And thou shalt have joy and **gladness**; and many shall rejoice at his birth.

1:44: For, lo, as soon as the voice of thy salutation sounded in mine ears, the babe leaped in my womb for **joy.**

ACTS

2:46: And they, continuing daily with one accord in the temple, and breaking bread from house to house, did eat their meat with **gladness** and singleness of heart.

HEBREWS

1:9: Thou hast loved righteousness, and hated iniquity; therefore God, even thy God, hath anointed thee with the oil of **gladness** above thy fellows.

JUDE

1:24: Now unto him that is able to keep you from falling, and to present you faultless before the presence of his glory with exceeding **joy.**

CHOROS

CHOROS – (Dancing) *A ring; a round dance; chorus; dancing; a company of dancers and singers; a circular dance; a choir.*

LYNN M. HAYDEN

LUKE

15:25: Now his elder son was in the field: and as he came and drew nigh to the house, he heard musick and **dancing.**

EXALLOMAI

EXALLOMAI – (Leaping) *To spring forth; to leap up.*

ACTS

3:8: And he **leaping up** stood, and walked, and entered with them into the temple, walking, and leaping, and praising God.

HALLOMAI

HALLOMAI – **(Spring; Leap)** *To jump; to spring forth; to leap up; to gush as a fountain.*

JOHN

4:14: But whosoever drinketh of the water that I shall give him shall never thirst; but the water that I shall give him shall be in him a well of water **springing** up into everlasting life.

ACTS

3:8: And he leaping up stood, and walked, and entered with them into the temple, walking, and **leaping,** and praising God.

14:10: Said with a loud voice, Stand upright on thy feet. And he **leaped** and walked.

ORCHEOMAI

ORCHEOMAI – **_(Dance)_** _(From Greek Orchos) To dance in rank or regular motion; a row or ring; to put in rapid motion; a line dance; artistic._

MATTHEW

11:17: And saying, We have piped unto you, and ye have not **danced**; we have mourned unto you, and ye have not lamented.

14:6: But when Herod's birthday was kept, the daughter of Herodias **danced** before them, and pleased Herod.

MARK

6:22: And when the daughter of the said Herodias came in, and **danced**, and pleased Herod and them that sat with him, the king said unto the damsel, Ask of me whatsoever thou wilt, and I will give it thee.

LUKE

7:32: They are like unto children sitting in the marketplace, and calling one to another, and saying, We have piped unto you, and ye have not **danced**; we have mourned to you, and ye have not wept.

PROCHORUS

PROCHORUS – (Prochorus' Name) *Pro-leader; cho-rus—dancer; therefore a dance leader or choreographer.*

LYNN M. HAYDEN

ACTS

6:5: And the saying pleased the whole multitude: and they chose Stephen, a man full of faith and of the Holy Ghost, and Philip, and **Prochorus**, and Nicanor, and Timon, and Parmenas, and Nicolas a proselyte of Antioch:

PROSKUNEO

PROSKUNEO – (Worship) *To prostrate oneself in homage; to kiss the Master's hand. It is a physical demonstration of total, intimate, spiritual abandonment, showing our sacrificial love to Him through the movement of humble prostration.*

MATTHEW

4:9: And saith unto him, All these things will I give thee, if thou wilt fall down and **worship** me.

4:10: Then saith Jesus unto him, Get thee hence, Satan: for it is written, Thou shalt **worship** the Lord thy God, and him only shalt thou serve.

8:2: And, behold, there came a leper and **worshipped** him, saying, Lord, if thou wilt, thou canst make me clean.

9:18: While he spake these things unto them, behold, there came a certain ruler, and **worshipped** him, saying, My daughter is even now dead: but come and lay thy hand upon her, and she shall live.

14:33: Then they that were in the ship came and **worshipped** him, saying, Of a truth thou art the Son of God.

15:25: Then came she and **worshipped** him, saying, Lord, help me.

JOHN

4:23: But the hour cometh, and now is, when the true worshippers shall **worship** the Father in spirit and in truth: for the Father seeketh such to **worship** him.

12:20: And there were certain Greeks among them that came up to **worship** at the feast:

ACTS

8:27: And he arose and went: and, behold, a man of Ethiopia, an eunuch of great authority under Candace queen of the Ethiopians, who had the charge of all her treasure, and had come to Jerusalem for to **worship**.

REVELATION

4:10: The four and twenty elders fall down before him that sat on the throne, and **worship** him that liveth for ever and ever, and cast their crowns before the throne, saying,

5:14: And the four beasts said, Amen. And the four and twenty elders fell down and **worshipped** him that liveth for ever and ever.

7:11: And all the angels stood round about the throne, and about the elders and the four beasts, and fell before the throne on their faces, and **worshipped** God.

SKIRTAO

SKIRTAO – (Leap) *To jump; move; leap for joy.*

LUKE

1:41: And it came to pass, that, when Elisabeth heard the salutation of Mary, the babe **leaped** in her womb; and Elisabeth was filled with the Holy Ghost:

1:44: For, lo, as soon as the voice of thy salutation sounded in mine ears, the babe **leaped** in my womb for joy.

6:23: Rejoice ye in that day, and **leap** for joy: for, behold, your reward is great in heaven: for in the like manner did their fathers unto the prophets.

CONCLUSION

Whether you have numerous studies about DANCE in the English vernacular (from both the old and new testaments); or participate in innumerable scripture studies about DANCE (derived from the Old Testament Hebrew); or do a comprehensive study of DANCE (from the New Testament Greek), I trust that you will have gained and continue to gain much wisdom, insight, and revelation. By the power of the Holy Spirit, may the anointing break the bonds of wickedness, heal the sick and brokenhearted, and cause many to come to a saving knowledge of Jesus Christ, as you DANCE, DANCE, DANCE!!!

Index

The following is a quick reference guide to some of the definitions for the Hebrew, Greek, and English words. Please refer to the appropriate page for the complete definition and scriptures.

Circular Dance 113

Dance Company 69

Dance Leader 121

Dancing. 65

Give Thanks 101

Glad or Joyful 111

Go Around 65

Gush as a Fountain 117

Jump for joy 43

Kiss the master's hand 123

Kneeling; Bowing 25

Leaping. 75

Many Hands Praising 97

Move 127

Perfume of Fire 91

Praise; Foolish 53

Procession; Feast. 33

Prostrate in Worship. 81

Put in Rapid Motion 119

Revolve; Surround 27

Rhythm. 17

Shake off; Terrify 73

Spin; Be Joyful 45

Spring Forth 117

Spring; Leap 41

Stamp; Skip 77

Strolling Minstrel 85

Travail; Whirl 37

Walking; Caravan 63

BIBLIOGRAPHY

Spirit Filled Life Bible – New King James Version

Thomas Nelson Publishers – Nashville – Atlanta – London – Vancouver

Thomas Nelson, Inc. 1991

General Editor – Jack W. Hayford, Litt.D.

Old Testament Editor – Sam Middlebrook, D.Min.

New Testament Editor – Jerry Horner, Th.D.

Assistant Editor – Gary Matsdorf, M.A.

Webster's New World Dictionary of the American Language

Simon and Schuster, a division of Gulf and Western Corp. 1982

1230 Avenue of the Americas

New York, New York 10020

The Exhaustive Concordance of the Bible

Abingdon Press, Nashville Forty-second Printing 1983

James Strong Madison, NJ

Key Word Comparison copyright 1980 by Abingdon

Blue Letter Bible. 1996-2002. Searched in 2006.

www.blueletterbible.org

CONTACT INFORMATION

Dancing For Him Ministries, Inc.

For further information about workshops, conferences, speaking engagements, videos, and ordering more books, etc., please feel free to contact us at:

info@dancingforhim.com
www.dancingforhim.com